All About Bottlenose Dolphins

By
Abby Quinn

Copyright 2022 Abby Quinn. All rights reserved.

This book is intended for education and entertainment purposes only. Under no circumstances does the author recommend that anyone should approach or handle any wild animal without expert supervision.

All pictures included in this book are pictures in the public domain, free for commercial use, or legally purchased stock photos. All information found in this book has been carefully researched and has been thoroughly checked for accuracy.

Table of Contents

Introduction 5

Classification 7

    The Five Traits of Mammals 9

Species 13

    Atlantic Bottlenose Dolphin 14

    Indo-Pacific Bottlenose Dolphin 15

Body structure 17

Snout and Teeth 23

Skin 26

Diet 28

Hunting Techniques 30

Breathing 35

Echolocation 38

Communication 41

Social Structure 43

Babies, Reproduction, and Life Cycle 47

Intelligence 51

Lifespan 54

Predators 56

Relationship With Humans 59

    Military Dolphins 60

Range 63

Population and Conservation Status 64

Threats 66

Books By Abby Quinn

Fiction

David and the Dream Dragon

Non-Fiction

All About Snakes   All About Crocodilians

All About Red Foxes   All About Lions

All About Komodo Dragons All About Tigers

All About Manatees   All About Bald Eagles

All About Animals Box Set #1

All About Polar Bears   All About Elephants

All About Giant Pandas   All About Snowy Owls

Non-Fiction (For Younger Kids)

All About Woodland Animals: Illustrated Animal Facts

All About Ocean Animals: Illustrated Animal Facts

Introduction

Bottlenose dolphins are one of the most popular, beloved animals on the face of the planet. Who doesn't love dolphins? They are beautiful, playful, and curious creatures. They are also extremely intelligent, and many experts consider them the second-smartest animal on Earth, after humans.

There are over 40 species of dolphin, but bottlenose dolphins are the most well-known species. They have appeared in countless movies and TV shows, and they are found in aquariums and marine parks all over the world!

Bottlenose dolphins are fascinating animals. They have complex social structures, are capable of communicating with each other and with humans, and they can perform complicated tasks and tricks.

Bottlenose dolphins are a common sight throughout the world's oceans. Unfortunately, coming into close contact with humans often puts them in danger. Keep reading to learn more about these beautiful animals, and how you can help protect them from harm.

Classification

What exactly is a dolphin?

Dolphins are **cetaceans**, a group of animals that also includes whales and porpoises.

There are two different types of dolphins—oceanic dolphins (which live in salt water) and freshwater dolphins, which live in fresh water.

Bottlenose dolphins are members of the *Delphinidae* family—the ocean-dwelling dolphins.

At first glance, dolphins might appear to be fish. After all, they spend their entire lives in the ocean, just like fish, and cannot live on land. There are other traits that they share with fish, too, and many people have made the mistake of assuming that dolphins are fish. But the truth is, dolphins are **mammals**, just like humans!

The Five Traits of Mammals

There are five traits that all mammals share, and dolphins have all of them. (We'll go over some of these traits in greater detail in later chapters, but for now, here's a brief overview.)

1.) Warm-blooded. All mammals are warm-blooded. What this means is that mammals are capable of regulating their own body temperature, and do not rely on external factors (like warmth or sunlight) to keep a stable internal temperature. Another word for warm-blooded is **endothermic**. Endothermic animals can keep a stable body temperature that is usually higher than their environment. Like all mammals, dolphins are warm-blooded. Most fish are cold-blooded.

2.) Body hair. All mammals have hair on their bodies at some point in their lives. Some mammals have lots of hair, and others have very little. Dolphins appear to be completely smooth and hairless...and they are. However, when dolphins are born, they do have a little bit of body hair! It falls out as the dolphin grows, and they never regrow the hair.

3.) They breathe air. All mammals breathe air through lungs. Fish, on the other hand, use gills to extract oxygen straight from the water. Dolphins have lungs, not gills, and even though they live in the water, they must return to the surface every so often to breathe, or they'll drown.

4.) Milk. Mammals produce milk to feed their newborn babies. Some of the other "mammalian" traits can be shared with other groups of animals. But the ability to produce milk is a trait that is completely unique to mammals! Mother dolphins feed their babies with milk, just like other mammals.

5.) Live birth. Most animals on Earth do not give birth to live young; they lay eggs, and the babies hatch from the eggs. But almost every single mammal gives birth to live young instead. There are a very few mammals that lay eggs, but they are exceptions to the rule, and dolphins are not one of them—baby dolphins are born live, not hatched from eggs.

Most mammals live on land. They are specially adapted for walking and breathing air. So how did dolphins end up in the ocean in the first place?

Dolphins evolved from a four-legged, land-dwelling mammal that lived over 50 million years ago. The name of this animal was *Pakiectus*, and it was also a very distant relative of modern-day hippos. It lived near the water, and it began to physically adapt to living in an aquatic environment. Over millions of years, these prehistoric mammals lost their limbs and evolved other traits that allowed them to survive underwater, and they eventually evolved into the bottlenose dolphins that we know and love today!

Did You Know?

A male dolphin is called a bull, a female is called a cow, and a baby is called a calf!

Species

For a long time, bottlenose dolphins were considered to be just one species. But in the early 2000's, more thorough research revealed that there are actually two species: the Atlantic bottlenose dolphin and the Indo-Pacific bottlenose dolphin.

The two types of bottlenose dolphin are very similar to each other, with only slight differences in size and appearance. The real difference between them is where they are found. The Indo-Pacific dolphin only lives in certain parts of the Indian Ocean and Pacific Ocean, while the Atlantic dolphin can be found throughout the world.

Atlantic Bottlenose Dolphin

Atlantic bottlenose dolphins are the larger of the two species, and they have shorter snouts.

The Atlantic bottlenose dolphin is also known as the common bottlenose dolphin. This dolphin is the more well-known of the two species due to its popularity in captivity; if you've seen a dolphin in an aquarium or a marine park, the chances are very good that it was an Atlantic bottlenose dolphin.

Atlantic bottlenose dolphins are larger than Indo-Pacific dolphins; they can weigh over 1,000 pounds, but an average weight of 500-600 is more common. They can be anywhere from 6 to 12 feet long!

The Atlantic bottlenose dolphin's scientific name is *Tursiops truncates*.

Indo-Pacific Bottlenose Dolphin

The main way to identify an Indo-Pacific bottlenose dolphin is to look at its snout. These dolphins have longer, thinner snouts than the common bottlenose dolphin.

The Indo-Pacific bottlenose dolphin was only recently classified as its own species. It is smaller than its common Atlantic cousin, and has a slenderer body. Its snout is also thinner and longer than the Atlantic dolphin's, and it has more teeth.

Indo-Pacific dolphins also have gray or black spots on their sides and underbellies, and is often a lighter shade of gray.

Indo-Pacific dolphins tend to stick close to coasts and shorelines, and rarely venture into the open ocean—unlike the Atlantic bottlenose dolphin.

They are usually around 8 ½ feet long and weigh around 500 pounds.

The Indo-Pacific bottlenose dolphin's scientific name is *Tursiops aduncus*.

Body Structure

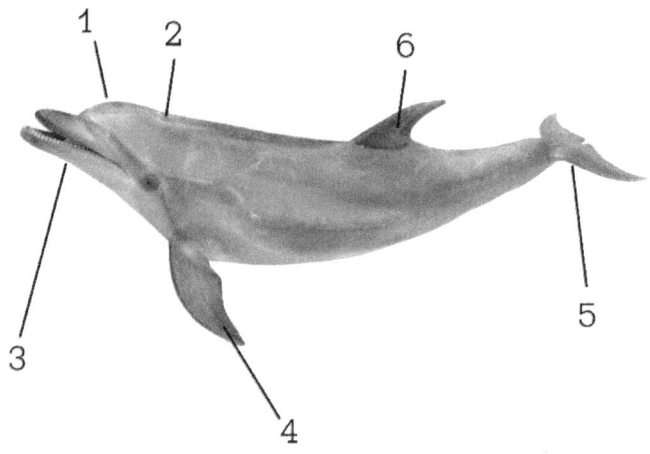

The body parts of a bottlenose dolphin. 1.) Melon 2.) Blowhole 3.) Snout (or rostrum) 4.) Pectoral flippers 5.) Tail flukes 6.) Dorsal fin

Bottlenose dolphins have slim, streamlined bodies. They have a specialized body shape called a **fusiform body**. Animals with fusiform bodies are slightly torpedo-shaped, with a narrow head, a wider body, and a narrow tail. This special shape reduces drag in the water and enables fast swimming, especially in open water. Many ocean-dwelling animals have fusiform bodies, especially fast-swimming predators like sharks and barracudas.

Bottlenose dolphins have the same basic body structure as other dolphins. They have a snout (called a rostrum), a dorsal fin, a melon, a tail ending in two flukes, a blowhole, and two pectoral flippers.

The blowhole, the melon, and the rostrum will all be discussed in other chapters, since they're important to other functions like breathing and eating. But for now, let's discuss the body parts that enable dolphins to swim—the **pectoral flippers**, the **dorsal fin**, and the **flukes**. Each of these parts work hand-in-hand to maximize the dolphin's underwater speed and mobility.

These three body parts also serve another crucial function—temperature regulation. The flippers, dorsal fin, and tail are filled with veins and arteries. By controlling the amount of blood that is pumped to these blood vessels, the dolphin can conserve body heat in extreme cold, or shed excess heat when it's too hot! This is essential for survival, since dolphins cannot sweat, and so they need a way to safely maintain their body temperature.

Pectoral Flippers

Dolphins only have two limbs—the pectoral flippers. They are the forelimbs; their "arms". Each flipper is about 1 ½ feet long and is shaped like an oar, with a slight backward curve and a pointed tip.

The pectoral flippers function like a combination of a rudder and a brake; the dolphins use them to steer and to stop! Without their flippers, dolphins wouldn't be able to control their speed or direction while swimming.

Did You Know?

Of course, dolphins don't have fingers. Their flippers are one smooth, solid surface. But a look at an x-ray reveals something remarkable—the bones in a dolphin's flippers resemble the bones in our hand. They have "wrist" and "finger" bones, although three of these "fingers" are very short. These bones are leftovers from before dolphins evolved to live in water.

Dorsal Fin

Bottlenose dolphins have a special fin, called a dorsal fin, in the middle of their backs. This fin is triangular-shaped and is usually curved backwards, but can also be straight in some cases.

There are no bones or muscle in this fin. Instead, it is filled with dense connective tissue. Since this fin contains no muscle, the dolphins cannot move it.

Its main purpose is to provide balance and stability in the water. It works just like a keel or a leeboard on a ship!

Of the three main external body parts, the dorsal fin is probably the least important for survival. Bottlenose dolphins with severe dorsal fin injuries can usually survive in the wild without human assistance.

Tail

Bottlenose dolphins have long, powerful tails. The tail ends in two long, flat fins called **flukes**. There are no bones in the flukes, but they are made of tendons and connective tissue that keeps the flukes rigid.

Dolphins use their tails to swim. They move their tails up and down, which creates momentum and propels them through the water. The flukes work just like paddles.

In summary, all parts of a dolphin's body work together to allow it to move through the water. The tail gives it raw swimming power, the pectoral flippers allow it to steer and stop, and the dorsal fin gives it balance and stability!

Did You Know?

Bottlenose dolphins have a cruising speed of around 5-6 miles per hour. However, when they need to, they can reach a top speed of over 20 miles per hour!

Snout and Teeth

Bottlenose dolphins get their name from the shape of their snouts! These dolphins have a short, bluntly rounded, bottle-shaped snout that is actually called a **rostrum**.

Of course, the word "bottlenose dolphin" isn't quite correct. The dolphin's rostrum isn't a nose at all; its actual nose is located on top of its head, and is called a blowhole.

Bottlenose dolphins use their snouts to forage for food on the bottom of the seafloor, and also as weapons when they must defend themselves against predators. They have a very unique defense system against sharks in particular; there is a thick layer of bone under the rostrum, which makes the snout very strong and tough. When a group of dolphins is threatened by a shark, they will dart through the water very quickly and slam into the shark with their jaws closed. The snout works like a battering ram, and dolphins have been known to kill sharks by literally battering them to death using their snouts.

Their snouts are very useful tools against predators, but for prey dolphins have a more important weapon—teeth.

Bottlenose dolphins have a lot of teeth; anywhere from 72 to 104, depending on the dolphin's health, species, and age. Their teeth are pointed and are shaped like a cone. They are sharp, but slightly blunted, and these teeth are perfect for gripping slippery fish—the bottlenose dolphin's favorite prey.

Many mammals (including humans) have teeth of different shapes and sizes, because each of these teeth serve a different function. For instance, canine teeth are sharp and meant for ripping into meat, and molars are flat and are used to grind food.

But bottlenose dolphins have teeth that are all the same shape and size! This is because their teeth serve only one purpose—to hold onto prey. The dolphins don't chew their food; they swallow it whole, and so they have no need for canine teeth or molars.

Did You Know?

Unlike humans, dolphins don't have two sets of teeth. Baby dolphins are born toothless, and their adult teeth come in after a few months. They only have one set of teeth, and if a dolphin loses a tooth, it cannot be replaced.

Skin

The skin of a bottlenose dolphin is smooth, sleek, and hairless (at least in adults; baby bottlenose dolphins do have a little bit of body hair). It has a rubber-like texture, and it's very thick; almost twenty times thicker than the skin of most mammals!

Its skin serves a very important purpose—protection. Dolphins have no body hair to keep them warm, and no sweat glands to keep them cool; their thick skin protects them from both extreme heat and extreme cold.

It's not uncommon to see a bottlenose dolphin with lots of scars and deep scratches on its skin. Sometimes these scratches are inflicted by other dolphins, either through fighting or playing. Sometimes the scars are from encounters with predators, like sharks. And sometimes they're wounded by manmade structures, such as fishing nets. But the skin of a bottlenose dolphin is so thick that it's able to withstand most surface injuries.

The skin of a bottlenose dolphin is either dark gray or light gray. This gray color gradually fades to very light gray or white on the bottom of the dolphin's belly. Bottlenose dolphins that live near coastlines tend to be lighter than dolphins that live in the open ocean.

Underneath the dolphin's skin is a thick layer of **blubber**. Blubber is fatty tissue, and it is vital to living in water; nearly every marine mammal has blubber! A bottlenose dolphin's blubber has many uses. It keeps the dolphins warm, which is extremely important in colder waters. It also helps the dolphins float, which makes swimming much easier and more energy-efficient. And finally, it serves as an emergency energy source when the dolphins can't find food.

The layer of blubber can be up to 2 inches thick, and can make up 20 percent of the dolphin's total body weight!

Diet

Bottlenose dolphins are carnivores, which means that they eat meat. But they are a special type of carnivore—a hypercarnivore. **Hypercarnivores** are animals that eat exclusively meat. Unlike some carnivores, like wolves, dolphins haven't been known to eat any plants at all.

Bottlenose dolphins feed on a variety of animals, but their favorite prey by far is fish. They eat dozens of species of small and medium-sized fish; since bottlenose dolphins can be found all over the world, the species they eat depends on their location. Some of their favorite fish include smelt, mackerel, herring, and mullet.

Bottlenose dolphins eat a lot—up to 22 pounds of fish per day!

While they prefer fish, bottlenose dolphins will also eat other animals. They prefer eating prey with soft bodies, such as octopuses, squids, and shrimp. They will also eat jellyfish; although jellyfish aren't as nutritious as fish or squid, and the dolphins only seem to eat them when their favorite prey is scarce.

Bottlenose dolphins can't chew their food; they swallow it whole, and so they prefer prey that is soft and small enough to swallow. If a dolphin catches a fish that is too big to swallow whole, it will fling the fish against a hard object (such as a rock or large piece of coral), or against the surface of the water, until the fish breaks up into small enough pieces to swallow.

Hunting Techniques

Bottlenose dolphins work together to catch fish.

A bottlenose dolphin's greatest strength is its high intelligence and its highly sociable nature. Bottlenose dolphins work together to hunt—by using teamwork and complex techniques, they make sure that every dolphin in the group has enough to eat.

First, the group of hungry dolphins must find their prey. They often hunt in water that is dark or murky, so instead of relying solely on their eyesight, they use echolocation to find fish.

Bottlenose dolphins prefer to hunt fish that gather in large schools. One of the most common hunting techniques that bottlenose dolphins use is called the **bait ball technique**. The dolphins swim around a school of fish, herding them into a tight ball. Then, the dolphins take turns darting through the ball, snatching up the fish at their leisure. Whenever the fish try to swim away, the dolphins herd them into a ball again. They do this over and over, until each dolphin has had a chance to eat their fill.

The bait ball technique is very successful, and most bottlenose dolphins prefer to use it whenever possible. But it works best in the deep water of the open ocean. When hunting in shallower waters, there are other techniques that work better.

In a technique known as **strand feeding**, the dolphins will drive a school of fish towards a beach, sandbar, or muddy flat. The fish jump out of the water to avoid the dolphins and get stuck on land. In order to get the fish, the dolphins have to "strand" themselves by pushing their bodies out of the water and onto dry land, where they snatch up the fish. The dolphins then free themselves by wiggling their bodies and sliding back into the water.

Not all bottlenose dolphins can use the strand feeding technique. It is a **learned behavior**, which means that it isn't part of the dolphin's natural hunting instincts; it's something that they teach each other! If a group of dolphins has mastered strand feeding, they will pass it on to their offspring, who will in turn teach it to *their* offspring.

Did You Know?

When using the strand feeding technique, bottlenose dolphins always strand themselves on their right side, not the left. Scientists aren't sure why.

Dolphins don't always hunt in groups! Sometimes they hunt alone. One of the most common solo strategies is **crater feeding**. The dolphin will dart down to the ocean floor and snatch up unsuspecting prey from above. It is called "crater feeding" from the small "crater" that is left in the ocean floor from the force of the dolphin swimming downward.

Individual dolphins will sometimes smack fish with their tails. This stuns the fish so they cannot move; the dolphin then snatches up the fish.

On the lower Florida coast, a very remarkable behavior has been seen amongst the bottlenose dolphins that hunt in the shallow waters—**mud ring feeding**. First, a group of dolphins find a school of fish. Then, one dolphin will swim around the school close to the bottom of the sea floor, moving its tail up and down. This creates a dense cloud of muddy water that works like a net to trap the fish in a circle. The fish get disoriented and try to jump out of the mud ring—straight into the waiting jaws of the other dolphins.

Mud ring feeding is fascinating to marine biologists because it is a relatively new behavior. It is also a learned behavior, and at first only a small group of dolphins in Florida were known to use it. But now it is slowly spreading, and dolphins as far away as the Caribbean have been observed using this technique!

Breathing

Most ocean animals get the oxygen that they need to survive straight from the water. Fish have gills that that filter oxygen from the water, while some invertebrates like starfish absorb oxygen through their skin. These animals never have to come up to the surface to breathe, and can live their lives completely submerged in water.

But dolphins, like all mammals, breathe air. Although they spend their entire lives in the water, they must come up to the surface to breathe.

Bottlenose dolphins need to breathe at least once every few minutes. They can hold their breath for up to 10-12 minutes at a time, but they generally breathe more often than that.

Dolphins have a hole on top of their heads called a **blowhole**. The blowhole is the dolphin's nose; it's on top of its head, not at the end of its snout! The blowhole is covered by a strong, muscular flap that closes when the dolphin dives underwater; this flap creates a seal that prevents any water from getting inside the blowhole.

To take a breath, the dolphin swims up to the surface, opens its blowhole, and exhales the air trapped in its lungs. After it inhales, it closes the flap over the blowhole before it dives underwater again.

Because they must breathe every few minutes, dolphins usually don't dive too deep in search of food. They can't risk being trapped underwater and being unable to return to breathe. They ordinarily dive about 30 feet under the water, but can dive 150 feet or more if they need to.

Land mammals (like humans, for example) breathe involuntarily; which means we do it without thinking about it. For us, breathing is an automatic function—which is why we can breathe even when we're asleep. But dolphins cannot breathe involuntarily; if they did, they would drown. Each breath they take is a deliberate act.

But how, then, do dolphins breathe when they are asleep?

Well, dolphins don't sleep...at least, not like we do. Dolphins experience a type of sleep called **unihemispheric sleep**. This means that only one side of the dolphin's brain sleeps at a time! While half of the brain is asleep, the other half stays awake and controls its basic bodily functions—so even when sleeping, the dolphin can still swim, breathe, and watch its surroundings.

A bottlenose dolphin spends around 30 percent of its day sleeping. When sleeping, it stays close to the surface and doesn't move around very much. When one half of its brain is rested, the dolphin will switch, and the other half will sleep, until both halves are fully rested.

Did You Know?

Dolphins literally sleep with one eye open! One eye stays open, watching for danger, while the other one stays closed.

Echolocation

A dolphin's forehead and its lower jaw both play an important role in echolocation.

Echolocation is probably the bottlenose dolphin's most unique and useful ability! It's an important part of the dolphin's hunting strategies, and it plays a role in navigation, communication, and socialization.

Echolocation is the ability to locate far-away objects by using sound instead of sight. This is especially useful for detecting things in dimness or even complete darkness. Echolocation is a rather rare ability. Only a few animals can use it: toothed whales, bats, some species of birds and shrews—and, of course, dolphins!

But how exactly does echolocation work?

Dolphins have a body part called a **melon**. The melon is a large mass of tissue that is located on the dolphin's forehead, between its blowhole and its rostrum. It's filled with fat and fluid, and is soft and flexible to the touch. This fatty lump may not look like much, but it's essential to both echolocation and communication!

Dolphins produce a wide variety of sounds through their nasal passages. The sound travels through the nasal passages, then through the melon, which acts like a "lens" to both intensify the sound and to focus it in a straight line.

When the sound waves hit an object in the water, they bounce back to the dolphin, rather like an echo (which is how "echolocation" got its name). The dolphin's lower jaw is also filled with fat and fluid, and the sound wave is absorbed by the lower jaw and into the inner ear. From there, the dolphin can process the information and form an image in its head!

Echolocation is a very powerful and effective ability. Using only sound waves, dolphins can detect an object as small as a golf ball over very long distances. They can "see" underwater objects up to 650 feet away! However, echolocation is most effective at shorter ranges.

Dolphins use echolocation to find prey, avoid underwater obstacles, and detect potential predators. It's one of their most useful abilities, and one of the things that make dolphins truly unique animals.

Communication

Bottlenose dolphins are highly social animals, and they communicate with each other very effectively.

Dolphins can produce a wide range of sounds—most of them are either clicks or whistles. Dolphins don't have vocal cords like humans do, so their sounds are produced in the nasal cavity.

Dolphins use different combinations of clicks and whistles to locate each other, greet other dolphins, coordinate hunting strategies, and avoid physical confrontation.

Each dolphin has a **signature whistle.** This is a high-pitched, distinctive whistle that is unique to each dolphin. This whistle is used to identify themselves to other dolphins. The signature whistle is the dolphin's name!

There is a theory that dolphins have a complex, structured language—just like we do. However, there isn't any evidence (so far) to support this theory. But marine biologists agree that dolphin communication is still fascinating to study. While we can't understand what *they're* saying, they can (to some extent, at least) understand what *we're* saying! Dolphins in captivity can learn to follow complicated spoken commands.

Social Structure

Dolphins live in groups called **pods**. It was once thought that these pods were rigid, mostly unchanging social structures (like packs of wolves or herds of elephants). But recent research has revealed that the social lives of bottlenose dolphins are more complicated than we once believed.

Bottlenose dolphin pods are **fission-fusion societies**. This means that the pods are fluid and changing, and the dolphins may leave the pod and join another—sometimes several times in the same day! Unlike other animals that live in groups, (again, like wolves or elephants) all the dolphins in the pod aren't always related to each other.

Dolphins are one of the few animals that are proven to form friendships with each other! Dolphins have friends, and they sometimes travel together from pod to pod.

The number of dolphins in a pod can vary greatly depending on a number of factors. However, bottlenose dolphin pods in the deep water of the open ocean tend to be larger than dolphin pods in shallower water near coastlines.

Bottlenose dolphin pods are complex and ever-changing, but in general, there are three types of pods.

1.) Nursery pods. These are groups of pregnant dolphins, nursing mothers and their young calves, and mothers with near-grown calves. They band together for support and protection. The non-nursing mothers and their older calves will protect the smaller, weaker members of the pod. These pods usually consist of 5 to 20 dolphins.

2.) Juvenile pods. These are groups of dolphins that are old enough to live on their own, but aren't fully mature yet. These groups consist of both male and female dolphins; which is remarkable, since adult male and female dolphins rarely live together full-time in the wild. The juvenile pods are important to a dolphin's social development; it's here in the juvenile pods where bottlenose dolphins will finish up learning how to socialize and interact with each other. When the females in the pods reach adulthood, they will leave to join a nursery pod—usually their mother's!

Juveniles usually only interact with other juveniles, not adults, but sometimes juvenile females will leave the pod to briefly visit their mothers in the nursery pod.

3.) Male pods. These are smaller groups consisting only of males. Some males are solitary, but others form small pods of their own.

When a juvenile male is still in the juvenile pod, he will form a bond with another male. This is called a **pair bond**. This friendship lasts into adulthood, and when the two males become adults they leave the juvenile pod and form pods of their own. They will stick together for a very long time—sometimes for life.

Male pods are much smaller than other pods, and they travel more, too. They will sometimes swim on the outskirts of a larger pod, to provide protection or to get an easy meal, but rarely stick around for long. For the most part, they keep to themselves except for when it's time to mate.

The three pods (nursery, juvenile, and male) are the most common types of pods, but sometimes there are pods that don't quite fit any of the definitions above.

Sometimes many pods of dolphins can come together to create an enormous, temporary super-pod. These groups can consist of as many as 1,000 dolphins or more!

Babies, Reproduction, and Life Cycle

One of the defining characteristics of a mammal is the ability to give birth to live young, and to nurse the babies with milk!

A bottlenose dolphin is officially an adult when it is around 5 to 15 years old. Females usually mature more quickly than males.

A bottlenose dolphin's gestation period is around 12 months—a whole year! (A **gestation period** is the amount of time that an animal is pregnant, and the amount of time that it takes for a baby to develop inside its mother). Dolphins have very long gestation periods—a human's, for example, is only 9 months.

Bottlenose dolphins give birth to only one baby at a time. Twins are possible, but extremely rare—only a handful of cases have ever been reported.

Dolphin calves can be born at any time, but most of them are born in the spring or summer, when the water is warmer and they have the greatest chances of survival.

When it's time for a female dolphin to give birth, she separates herself from the rest of the pod and swims to a safe, quiet place in shallow water. Sometimes she gives birth alone, but other times another dolphin from the pod will stay with her to help and support her. These helper dolphins are sometimes called "auntie" dolphins; but these "aunties" can be male or female, and may not necessarily be related to the birthing dolphin. The auntie is the only other dolphin that a mother will allow near her while she is giving birth.

Most dolphin calves are born tail-first to prevent accidental drowning. As soon as the calf is born, the mother (and the auntie, if there is one) will push the baby to the surface of the water so it can take its first breath.

A newborn bottlenose dolphin weighs 20 to 40 pounds at birth, and is around 43 inches long. It is completely toothless when it is born, but unlike some mammals, it isn't born blind; it can see perfectly well from the moment it's born.

Newborn calves are slightly darker than adults, and they have several lightly-colored lines on their bodies. These lines are called **fetal folds** and are from where the calves were folded up while still in the womb. These markings help researchers identify newborn dolphins! The fetal folds vanish after a few months.

After the calf is born, it and its mother rejoin the pod. When the pod travels, small calves and their mothers swim in the middle, where they are protected by other dolphins on all sides.

A dolphin calf doesn't swim by its mother's side; it swims slightly behind her. When the mother swims, she creates a "slipsteam" in the water behind her. The calf swims directly in this current, when propels it forward. This helps the baby swim quickly with minimum effort, which ensures that it doesn't get too tired...and, more importantly, that it doesn't get left behind.

A mother dolphin and her calf have a very strong bond. Calves stay with their mothers for a very long time—three to six years on average. They usually stay even long after they stop nursing—calves are weaned when they are around 1 ½ to 2 years old.

Young bottlenose dolphins have a lot to learn! Over the next few years, the mothers (and other members of the pod) teach the babies how to hunt, how to communicate, and how to avoid danger.

When a dolphin calf is fully grown, it leaves its mother's pod and goes in search of a pod of its own. However, most dolphins will return to visit their mothers from time to time!

Intelligence

Bottlenose dolphins are highly intelligent animals. It's difficult to properly rank animal intelligence, but bottlenose dolphins are on the same intelligence level as elephants and apes. Some people even consider them the second most intelligent species on the planet, after humans.

All dolphins are intelligent, but the bottlenose dolphin is the smartest of them all!

Dolphins are extremely quick learners and top-notch problem solvers, and they can perform complex tasks. They're capable of teaching each other and learning new skills just by observing.

But their emotional intelligence is even more remarkable. Dolphins experience complex emotions like empathy and grief—emotions that few animals have.

Bottlenose dolphins have the second largest brain-to-body-size ratio of all animals—only humans have a larger brain in comparison to their body size. When you compare a human's brain and a dolphin's brain side-by-side, they look remarkably similar. The dolphin's brain has many creases and folds—the mark of high intelligence, since folded brains contain more neurons than smooth brains.

Bottlenose dolphins have special cells in their brains called **spindle cells**. These cells give the dolphins the ability to remember, adapt to change, communicate, and solve problems.

Dolphins are one of the few animals to possess **self-awareness**, which means that they are aware of themselves as individuals and can recognize themselves in a mirror! Only a handful of other animals have been proven to have self-awareness; some examples are apes, elephants, orcas, and magpies.

Bottlenose dolphins are one of the few animals to use tools! Some dolphins will use sea sponges to cover their snouts when they're foraging for food on the sea floor. The sponges protect their snouts from being scratched or scraped. This is another example of a learned behavior; only some dolphins do this, and they learn it from their mother.

In fact, bottlenose dolphins are so intelligent that some people believe that they shouldn't be classified as an animal at all, and should instead be considered "non-human people", and therefore be treated under law as unique individuals with rights and protection.

Lifespan

Dolphins and whales are well-known for having long lifespans, and bottlenose dolphins are no different. While they don't live as long as some whales (for instance, fin whales can live to be over 100 years old!), bottlenose dolphins still live remarkably long lives.

In the wild, bottlenose dolphins live for an average of 40 years, but it's not unusual for them to live to be 60. It's not clear why, but female dolphins live slightly longer than males, and females are more likely to live to the ripe old age of 60 than males are.

Most mammals live longer in captivity than in the wild...sometimes *much* longer. But dolphins are different; they live longer lives when they are free in the wild. Dolphins in captivity usually only live 13 to 25 years, although they can live longer. There isn't much data on the lifespans of bottlenose dolphins in the wild versus in captivity, but most of the data seems to agree that they do much better in the wild. However, in recent years, dolphins in aquariums and theme parks seem to be living longer than they did in the past. This is probably due to an increase in the quality of care the dolphins receive, as well as a better understanding of their unique social needs.

Predators

Sharks are one of the bottlenose dolphin's main predators.

The ocean is a treacherous place with numerous predators and a complex food chain...but dolphins rank very high on it! They have very few natural predators—however, because they are smaller in size than some other marine animals, they are sometimes targeted by large carnivores.

Sharks are the bottlenose dolphin's biggest threat. Great white sharks, tiger sharks, bull sharks, and other large sharks will attack and eat dolphins—especially the vulnerable calves.

However, dolphins are anything but easy prey. They may be small, but they use a combination of intelligence, speed, and teamwork to evade and outswim a hunting shark. If fleeing fails, the dolphins will attack. They swim underneath the shark and then rapidly dart upwards, ramming the shark's soft underbelly with their hard snouts. They do this until the shark flees, or until it dies from internal injuries.

This is a very effective strategy. In fact, many sharks will avoid a group of dolphins altogether, unless an opportunity for an easy meal presents itself.

Other than sharks (and humans, but we'll get to that later) the only other predator that poses a threat to dolphins is the orca. Orcas are also known as killer whales, but they aren't whales at all—they are actually the largest members of the dolphin family! They are fierce and formidable hunters, and they eat other marine mammals—even their smaller cousins, the bottlenose dolphins.

Orcas are nearly as intelligent as dolphins, and they have complex cooperative hunting strategies of their own. They are powerful, and swim just as quickly as dolphins do.

But bottlenose dolphins aren't the first choice of prey for either sharks or orcas. In most cases, the dolphins are more trouble than they're worth for these predators.

Relationship With Humans

Humans and bottlenose dolphins have interacted with each other for centuries, and in many cases, they even formed mutually beneficial relationships. Dolphins would sometimes work together with local fishermen, and would drive fish towards the fishermen's nets in exchange for a portion of the fish. This still happens today, especially in more remote parts of the world.

Bottlenose dolphins have a strong sense of empathy, and there are plenty of documented cases of bottlenose dolphins saving the life of a human! They will swim underneath an injured or drowning person and push them up to the surface, just as they do with each other when one of them is injured. There have even been cases of dolphins driving sharks away from humans.

Bottlenose dolphins have been kept in captivity for nearly 100 years. They are often the star attraction at zoos, aquariums, and marine parks, where they dazzle guests with their friendly dispositions and impressive tricks. There are hundreds of dolphins in captivity worldwide—perhaps even thousands.

Bottlenose dolphins are the most common dolphin kept in captivity.

Military Dolphins

Almost everyone knows that horses and dogs are trained by military and police forces to perform helpful tasks. But there is another government service animal that few people know about.

Both the United States Navy and the Russian military keep and train bottlenose dolphins to perform underwater tasks! These special dolphins are trained to locate underwater mines, find and retrieve lost equipment, locate lost swimmers, and protect ships from enemy divers.

The U.S Navy Marine Mammal Program is based in California, and it was started over 60 years ago, in the year 1960. In the program's early days, they experimented with nearly 20 different marine species, including birds and even sharks! Eventually, they settled on the two animals with the highest intelligence and trainability—the bottlenose dolphin and the California sea lion.

Military dolphins are trained by up to five separate expert teams, each one focusing on a specific task. The dolphins are very well-cared for, and are served by a team of marine biologists and veterinarians.

The bottlenose dolphin's high intelligence, along with its unique ability to use underwater sonar, make this animal invaluable to the military.

The U.S Navy also trains sea lions to perform similar tasks. Sea lions aren't quite as intelligent as bottlenose dolphins, and lack the ability to use echolocation, but they are still very smart, and they have excellent underwater vision.

The U.S Navy currently employs about 70 bottlenose dolphins and around 30 sea lions.

The Navy has stated that it does want to move away from using marine animals, and use underwater drones, artificial intelligence, and sonar instead. But right now, bottlenose dolphins are much more effective than drones; even the most sophisticated man-made technology can't quite match the dolphin's natural abilities!

Range

Bottlenose dolphins have an extremely wide range, and are a common sight both around coastlines and in the open ocean!

Despite their name, Atlantic bottlenose dolphins aren't just found in the Atlantic Ocean; in fact, they can be found in all the world's oceans— except for the two coldest oceans, the Arctic and the Antarctic oceans. They love warm, tropical, and sub-tropical waters, and they live in all types of marine habitats, like bays, gulfs, harbors, and deep open oceans. They can be found in nearly every country that shares a border with the ocean.

The Indo-Pacific bottlenose dolphin, however, is only found in certain areas. It mostly lives in the Indian Ocean, and in small parts of the western Pacific Ocean. Unlike its more common cousin, the Indo-Pacific dolphin does not like to live or travel in the open waters, and instead prefers to live near coastlines in warmer, shallower waters. It can be found off the coasts of India, China, eastern Africa, and northern Australia.

Population and Conservation Status

Wild bottlenose dolphins face many dangers and threats. But despite this, their population is still holding strong!

There are an estimated 600,000 Atlantic bottlenose dolphins left in the wild—although of course it's difficult to know the exact number. They are classified as Least Concern by conservation groups, which means that they are not in any immediate danger of extinction.

It's more difficult to assess the population numbers of Indo-Pacific bottlenose dolphins, because their range is scattered and they live in remote areas that are harder to conduct research in. However, they are classified as Near Threatened; which means that they aren't endangered yet, but may soon become endangered if the population doesn't begin to grow.

In short, the bottlenose dolphin population is healthy—but it's important to take steps to make sure that it stays that way.

Threats From Humans

Ocean pollution threatens dolphins and other marine life.

Bottlenose dolphins have very few natural predators, and they're intelligent enough to be able to avoid most dangers. However, there is one animal on Earth that threatens the existence of nearly all others—humans.

Bottlenose dolphins are one of the most beloved animals on Earth, and so they have protection from humans that most animals don't have. It is illegal in most countries to harm or kill a dolphin; in the United States, they are protected under the Marine Mammal Protection Act and any person who hurts or kills a bottlenose dolphin faces severe penalties, with a maximum fine of one hundred thousand dollars. Even without the law, in most parts of the United States (and many other countries) hunting a bottlenose dolphin is taboo.

Unfortunately, not all countries have banned the hunting of bottlenose dolphins. Some countries, such as Peru and Japan, still openly hunt dolphins for their meat, blubber, and skin. They are also often captured to be sold to aquariums and marine parks.

In some remote areas, the dolphins are protected by law, but they are still hunted because the laws aren't often enforced.

But the biggest threats from humans are indirect, not direct. Bottlenose dolphins are often negatively impacted by ocean pollution. They become tangled up in discarded fishing nets, which can affect their ability to swim; in severe cases, the dolphins become trapped and cannot swim to the surface, and so they drown.

Dolphins are impacted by chemical contamination and oil spills. They absorb these chemicals into their bodies, either directly or from eating contaminated fish. This can lead to deformities, cancer, infertility, and fatal illnesses.

Dolphins are very curious animals, and will often follow boats; this can lead to them being struck by boat propellers.

Bottlenose dolphins can be swept up in fishing nets (especially tuna fishing nets) where they are often drowned before the nets are pulled up to the surface.

While bottlenose dolphins aren't endangered, thousands of them are killed every year, and many conservationists worry that the dolphin population might soon decline.

How You Can Help

Anyone can help make the world a safer place for dolphins. Even small efforts can help a lot, especially if we all do them!

If you want to help save bottlenose dolphins (and other marine life) there are several things that you can do.

1) Clean up the beach. The next time you visit a beach, you can help dolphins by picking up and throwing away any litter that you see—especially glass, metal, fishing line, or fishing nets. Just a few moments of your time can make the ocean a cleaner, safer place for animals.

2.) Only buy dolphin-safe tuna. Look for the "dolphin-safe" label on tuna cans; this means that the company followed laws to minimize the number of dolphins that are trapped in tuna nets.

3.) Avoid wild dolphins. If you see a dolphin in the wild, you might be tempted to feed it or touch it; don't. Not only is it dangerous to approach any wild animal, but dolphins are very curious and social, and if they become too accustomed to people, they might become dependent on humans, and close contact with humans can put them in danger. Instead, observe them from a safe distance.

4) Avoid harmful products. Do your best to encourage your family to avoid buying single-use plastic items, such as Styrofoam plates, plastic bottles, and plastic bags. Many of these items end up in the ocean, where they can harm dolphins and other sea life. Instead, opt for reusable items, and recycle plastic containers whenever you can.

5.) Volunteer or donate. Many wildlife refuges, rescue organizations, and aquariums have programs that even children can volunteer for, and these programs directly benefit dolphins. You can also donate to rescue organizations or conservation groups.

If we all work together, we can make sure that the oceans remain a safe place for millions of marine animals, and that dolphins will be around for many years to come.

Author's Note

Thank you very much for reading!

This book, like all my books, is self-published, which means it was published without any help from agents or marketing experts. It's not easy to become established as a self-published author.

Therefore, if you enjoyed this book, please consider leaving a rating or review! Books are much more likely to be bought, borrowed, or talked about if they have lots of reviews. I also love receiving feedback from my readers.

Thank you for your support!

About The Author

Abby Quinn lives in the southern United States with her husband and daughter. Her passions are animals, nature, and books, and she's working hard on writing fiction books and on her non-fiction series.

To find out more about Abby Quinn's available books, visit her [Amazon.com Author Page](#).

Made in the USA
Las Vegas, NV
16 January 2024